# Women

# Of

# Courage

# The

# *OBSCURE*

# Bible Study Series

**Grow in your faith through investigating unusual biblical characters.**

### The OBSCURE Bible Study Series

| | |
|---|---|
| Meet Shamgar, Jethro, Manoah & Hathach | 4 Lessons |
| Blasphemy, Grace, Quarrels & Reconciliation | 8 Lessons |
| The Beginning and the End | 8 Lessons |
| God at the Center | 8 Lessons |
| Women of Courage | 8 Lessons |
| The Beginning of Wisdom | 8 Lessons |
| Miracles and Rebellion | 8 Lessons |
| The Chosen People | 8 Lessons |
| The Chosen Person | 8 Lessons |

# Women
# of
# Courage

**God did some serious business with these women.**

## Book 5 – Personal Study Guide

*Stephen H Berkey*

# COPYRIGHT

ISBN  978-1-952359-06-4    (Leader Guide, paperback)

ISBN  978-1-952359-07-1    (Leader Guide, ebook)

ISBN  978-1-952359-08-8    (Personal Study Guide, paperback)

ISBN  978-1-952359-09-5    (Personal Study Guide, ebook)

**Bible Translations Used:**

Unmarked scriptures and scriptures marked ESV are taken from THE HOLY BIBLE, ENGLISH STANDARD VERSION (ESV): Scriptures taken from THE HOLY BIBLE, ENGLISH STANDARD VERSION ® Copyright© 2001 by Crossway, a publishing ministry of Good News Publishers. Used by permission.

Scriptures marked NIV are taken from the NEW INTERNATIONAL VERSION (NIV): Scripture taken from THE HOLY BIBLE, NEW INTERNATIONAL VERSION ®. Copyright© 1973, 1978, 1984, 2011 by Biblica, Inc.™. Used by permission of Zondervan.

# RESOURCES

*Blessed is the one who finds wisdom, and the one who gets understanding.* (Proverbs 3:13 ESV)

You can access free resources from Get Wisdom by going to:

**www.getwisdom.link/resources**

You will always find:

1   Free Sample Study Lesson: "*Shamgar*" (PDF)

2   Free Worksheets for recording answers.
     For use by those who have an ebook or do not
     want to write in their hardcopy book.

You may find:

Other free materials that will be useful in your daily life, Bible study, or relationships.

# TABLE OF CONTENTS

*Title Pages* . . . . . . . . . . . . . . . . . . . . . . . . . . . . . . . . . . . . . . . . . . . . . . . . . . . . . . . . . . . . . *i*

*Copyright* . . . . . . . . . . . . . . . . . . . . . . . . . . . . . . . . . . . . . . . . . . . . . . . . . . . . . . . . . . . . . *iv*

*Resources* . . . . . . . . . . . . . . . . . . . . . . . . . . . . . . . . . . . . . . . . . . . . . . . . . . . . . . . . . . . . . *v*

*Table of Contents* . . . . . . . . . . . . . . . . . . . . . . . . . . . . . . . . . . . . . . . . . . . . . . . . . . . . . *vi*

*About the Leader Guide* . . . . . . . . . . . . . . . . . . . . . . . . . . . . . . . . . . . . . . . . . . . . . . . *vii*

*Why Study* OBSCURE *Characters?* . . . . . . . . . . . . . . . . . . . . . . . . . . . . . . . . . . *viii*

*Introduction* . . . . . . . . . . . . . . . . . . . . . . . . . . . . . . . . . . . . . . . . . . . . . . . . . . . . . . . . . . . . *ix*

*Now What?* . . . . . . . . . . . . . . . . . . . . . . . . . . . . . . . . . . . . . . . . . . . . . . . . . . . . . . . . . . . *107*

*The OBSCURE Bible Study Series* . . . . . . . . . . . . . . . . . . . . . . . . . . . . . . . . . . . *108*

*Acknowledgments* . . . . . . . . . . . . . . . . . . . . . . . . . . . . . . . . . . . . . . . . . . . . . . . . . . . . *110*

*Notes* . . . . . . . . . . . . . . . . . . . . . . . . . . . . . . . . . . . . . . . . . . . . . . . . . . . . . . . . . . . . . . . . . . *111*

*About the Author* . . . . . . . . . . . . . . . . . . . . . . . . . . . . . . . . . . . . . . . . . . . . . . . . . . . . *112*

*Key Points to Remember* . . . . . . . . . . . . . . . . . . . . . . . . . . . . . . . . . . . . . . . . . . . . . *113*

# CONTENTS

*Jael,* a peg in the head ................................................................01

*Gomer,* Hosea's promiscuous wife ................................................15

*Rizpah,* King Saul's concubine.......................................................29

*Woman of Tekoa,* who pretended to mourn ...............................43

*Tabitha,* Peter raised her from the dead .....................................57

*The Other Mary,* mother of James.................................................67

*Shiphrah & Puah,* midwives ...........................................................87

*Lydia,* dealer in purple cloth .........................................................97

# ABOUT THE LEADER GUIDE

All of the books in this Bible Study series have an extensive Leader Guide. If you are a participant in a group, a Leader Guide is not necessary, unless you want the author's answers. If you are studying independently, you may want the Leader Guide.

In the Guide the answers follow the questions with a small amount of space for the Leader's personal responses. If you are using the Leader Guide and want to do the study without the influence of the author's answers the best solution is to obtain the blank Worksheets, which are free. This will allow you to record your answers separately before reviewing the answers in the Leader Guide.

You can access the Worksheets by going to our website and entering your email address:

**www.getwisdom.link/resources**

# Why Study OBSCURE Characters?

### Unique, New, and Fresh

For experienced Bible students these characters will provide a fresh and interesting approach to Bible study. Since most of the material will be unfamiliar to the participants, new believers or those just starting Bible study should not feel intimidated by students who have been studying for years. Most readers will not be acquainted with the majority of the characters and events in this series.

### Knowledge of Scripture

These studies are a great introduction for those just beginning Bible study. Regardless of their level of knowledge, everyone should find the characters and stories provide an opportunity to grow in their faith through investigating fascinating and unusual biblical stories and incidents.

### Valuable Life Lessons

These lesser-known characters are a lot like you and me. God uses all sorts of people to accomplish His plans! You will become familiar with ordinary people, strange characters, and people living on the fringe of life who have the same troubles and challenges as people today. The deep truths and life lessons embedded in these studies should be valuable. They will provide new insights to scripture.

# INTRODUCTION

## Description of Series

This unique series uses a number of lesser-known Bible characters and events to explore such major themes as Angels, being Born Again, Courage, Death, Evangelism, Faithfulness, Forgiveness, Grace, Hell, Leadership, Miracles, the Remnant, the Sabbath, Salvation, Rebellion, Sovereignty, Thankfulness, Women, the World, Creation, and End Times.

The series as a whole provides both a broad and fresh understanding of the nature of God as we see Him act in the lives of people we've never examined before.

Most of the people chosen for these studies are unfamiliar because they are mentioned only a few times in Scripture – fifteen only once or twice. Others, although more familiar, are included because of their particular contribution to kingdom work.

For example, Scripture mentions Shamgar only twice. One verse in Judges 3:31 tells his story and 5:6 simply establishes a timeline and says nothing more about him. Then there is Nicodemus, with whom we associate the concept of being "born again." His name appears only 5 times, all in one short passage in the book of John. Eve, although obviously not obscure, is included in order to investigate the creation story.

## Book Description

Book 9 in the OBSCURE series is about the person Jesus Christ. We examine a number of characters closely associated with Jesus. The first is the priest Melchizedek. The primary focus of this lesson is on the superiority of Christ and the argument outlined in the book of Hebrews on that subject. We then examine one of the many scribes identified in the Bible. This is the scribe who said "I will follow you wherever you go," but Jesus questioned his priorities and his commitment.

Nicodemus is an interesting character because he was a Pharisee and he came at night seeking answers from Jesus. Jesus told Nicodemus that he had to be born again, but Nicodemus had difficulty understanding what Jesus was talking about.

Lazarus is the only character in any of the Biblical parables who is identified by name. He and a rich man had died and Lazarus was carried by the angels to Abraham's side. The rich man was in Hades. This story allows us to take an in-depth look at the subject of hell.

As we near the crucifixion the next lesson is Jesus on the cross with a criminal who knew who Jesus was and said, "Jesus, remember me when you come into your kingdom." Then Jesus made a remarkable promise: "Today you will be with me in Paradise."

Following the crucifixion Jesus appeared to two disciples walking home to Emmaus from Jerusalem. They had lost all hope and were deeply saddened by the events that had just taken place. Then Jesus joined them on the road, but they were kept from recognizing Him until he broke bread at the evening meal and blessed it.

The next subject is a gospel conversation, and we find Philip running down a dusty road to talk with an Ethiopian eunuch who had been in Jerusalem. Philip opened the conversation by asking, "How can I help?" and the result was that the eunuch later asked to be baptized.

Lastly, we look at the story in Acts describing Jason who hosted Paul and Silas in Thessalonica. Paul was being pursued and persecuted by the Jews and when they could not find Paul they took their anger out on Jason. This allows us to closely examine the subject of the Messiah.

## Group Discussion or Individual Study

These studies can be done individually or in a small discussion group. The real value of the study is in the discussion questions. We all see life differently and the thoughts and ideas shared in a group will often lead to a richer understanding of the Scripture. The questions often require the participant to put himself (herself) in the mind or circumstances of that person in the Scriptures.

The commentary portion of the introductory material in each lesson is there to help clarify the passage and set the stage for the discussion questions. The questions are designed to help the student understand the meaning of the text itself and explore the kingdom implications from a personal point of view.

## Ideal For Both New and Mature Bible Students

These lessons have three underlying questions:

- "Who is this person?"
- "What is happening here?"
- "What is the implication for my life?"

Because of the obscurity of the characters under study, chances are that even experienced participants with prior understanding of the lesson's theme will find fresh material to explore. Both new and long-time students will be challenged by the life lessons these unfamiliar characters can teach them.

## Format of Lessons

Each lesson begins with the Scripture using the ESV translation followed by short sections titled "Context," "What Do We Know," and "Observations." The discussion questions are designed to help the student understand the subject and are followed by several application questions.

## Format of Lessons

Each lesson begins with the Scripture using the ESV translation followed by short sections titled "Context," "What Do We Know," and "Observations." Discussion questions are generally organized by subject followed by four or five application question

# Women

# Of

# Courage

# *Jael*
## a peg in the head

---

**Occurrences of "Heber/Jael" in the Bible:** 5/6

**Themes:** Women; Courage

---

## Scripture

Judges 4:11-24
*Now Heber the Kenite had separated from the Kenites, the descendants of Hobab the father-in-law of Moses, and had pitched his tent as far away as the oak in Zaanannim, which is near Kedesh.*

*12 When Sisera was told that Barak the son of Abinoam had gone up to Mount Tabor, 13 Sisera called out all his chariots, 900 chariots of iron, and all the men who were with him, from Harosheth-hagoyim to the river Kishon. 14 And Deborah said to Barak, "Up! For this is the day in which the Lord has given Sisera into your hand. Does not the Lord go out before you?" So Barak went down from Mount Tabor with 10,000 men following him. 15 And the Lord routed Sisera and all his chariots and all his army before Barak by the edge of the sword. And Sisera got down from his chariot and fled away on foot. 16 And Barak pursued the chariots and the army to Harosheth-hagoyim, and all the army of Sisera fell by the edge of the sword; not a man was left.*

*17 But Sisera fled away on foot to the tent of Jael, the wife of Heber the Kenite, for there was peace between Jabin the king of Hazor* and the house of Heber the Kenite. 18 And Jael came out to meet Sisera and said to him, "Turn aside, my lord; turn aside to me; do not be afraid." So he turned aside to her into the tent, and she covered him with a rug. 19 And he said to her, "Please give me a little water to drink, for I am thirsty." So she opened a skin of milk and gave him a drink and covered him. 20 And he said to her, "Stand at the opening of the tent, and if any man comes and asks you, 'Is anyone here?' say, 'No.'" 21 But Jael the wife of Heber took a tent peg, and took a hammer in her hand. Then she went softly to him and drove the peg into his temple until it went down into the ground while he was lying fast asleep from weariness. So he died. 22 And behold, as Barak was pursuing Sisera, Jael went out to meet him and said to him, "Come, and I will show you the man whom you are seeking." So he went in to her tent, and there lay Sisera dead, with the tent peg in his temple.


23  So on that day God subdued Jabin the king of Canaan before the people of Israel. 24 And the hand of the people of Israel pressed harder and harder against Jabin the king of Canaan, until they destroyed Jabin king of Canaan. ESV


Judges 5:6, 24-27
"In the days of Shamgar, son of Anath, in the days of Jael, the highways were abandoned, and travelers kept to the byways. . . 24 Most blessed of women be Jael, the wife of Heber the Kenite, of tent-dwelling women most blessed. 25 He asked water and she gave him milk; she brought him curds in a noble's bowl. 26 She sent her hand to the tent peg and her right hand to the workmen's mallet; she struck Sisera; she crushed his head; she shattered and pierced his temple. 27 Between her feet he sank, he fell, he lay still; between her feet he sank, he fell; where he sank, there he fell— dead. ESV

## The Context:

The story of Heber and Jael occurs during the time of the Judges. Although Heber and Jael were not Judges, they lived during the time of Deborah, one of the major Judges of Israel. Deborah was the third of the major Judges following Othniel and Ehud. Her story follows that of Ehud and is told in chapters 4-5. During Deborah's time, Israel seemed frozen with inaction and was unable to unite to face their enemy from the North – Sisera, the commander of the Canaanite army.

Because of Israel's reluctance to face her enemies, Deborah struggled to get an organized response to Sisera's army. Barak would not follow Deborah's instruction to go to Mt. Tabor unless she went go along with him and Deborah said in 4:9 that the honor of the victory would not go to Barak, "for the Lord will sell Sisera into the hand of a woman." The woman was not identified.

This story is told first in a prose format in chapter 4 and then repeated in chapter 5 in what is usually called "The Song of Deborah." To get the entire story one must read both chapters.

## What Do We Know?

Barak's underlying problem is that he did not trust God. Fortunately, Deborah trusted that God would bring the victory even if Barak was reluctant. It was a form of rebuke when Deborah told Barak that a woman would be responsible for the victory. It would have brought shame for a warrior to rely on a woman in battle. For example:

> Judges 9:53-54
> *And a certain woman threw an upper millstone on*

> Abimelech's head and crushed his skull. 54 Then he called
> quickly to the young man his armor-bearer and said to him,
> "Draw your sword and kill me, lest they say of me, 'A
> woman killed him.'" And his young man thrust him through,
> and he died. ESV

Sisera, commander of King Jabin's forces, chose the Jezreel Valley
by the Kishon River as the battleground. There his chariots had
room to maneuver, but he was not protected from the storms and
floods of Almighty God:

> Judges 5:20-21      *From heaven the stars fought, from their*
> *courses they fought against Sisera. 21 The torrent Kishon*
> *swept them away, the ancient torrent, the torrent Kishon.*
> *March on, my soul, with might!* ESV

The story is a tale of allies, friends, traitors, and mixed loyalties.
Although the Kenites were originally allied with Israel, some or
many had moved north and supported the Canaanites. Thus, Heber
told Sisera that Barak was going to Mt. Tabor (4:12). The
relationship between Sisera and Heber is made clear in 4:17 where
it says the clan of Heber, the Kenite, had friendly relations with the
Canaanites.

But apparently Heber's wife Jael had not changed her loyalties, to
Sisera's distress!

## Implications and Observations

### ARMAGEDDON: the Jezreel Valley

Revelation 16:16    *And they assembled them at the place that in*
*Hebrew is called Armageddon.* ESV

Armageddon is traditionally considered to be the site of the final
battle of the church age in which God will destroy the armies of

Satan and throw him into the abyss (Rev 16:16; 20:1-3, 7-10). The word "Armageddon" is derived from Mt. Megiddo and is probably a reference to the location of the valley between Mount Carmel and the city of Jezreel. This is commonly known as the Valley of Jezreel, sometimes called the Plain of Esdraelon. The Jezreel Valley was an important trade route and had major highways going both east and west as well as north and south. Given the terrain and the importance of the travel routes it is not surprising that major battles occurred here.

It was the location of several disasters:

- Saul's death and Israel's defeat by the Philistines (1 Sam 31), and
- King Josiah's death in battle (2 Kings 23).

THE PEOPLE - OVERVIEW

- Jabin was a king in Canaan who reigned in Hazor.
- Sisera was commander of Jabin's army.
- Deborah was a Judge and prophetess who led Israel.
- Barak was the leader of Israel's army, who reported to Deborah.
- Heber was a Kenite (a descendant of Jethro).
    [Kenites had been associated with or aligned
        with Israel since the days of Moses]
- Heber and his wife Jael left the Kenites, and moved into Canaanite territory and aligned themselves with or became friends with the Canaanites.

## Discussion Questions

### A. GENERAL

A1. What do we learn about the Kenites in Judges 1:16?

Judges 1:16     *And the descendants of the Kenite, Moses' father-in-law, went up with the people of Judah from the city of palms into the wilderness of Judah, which lies in the Negeb near Arad, and they went and settled with the people.* ESV

A2. Jabin was the Canaanite king. What was the source of his power?

Judges 4:1-3     *And the people of Israel again did what was evil in the sight of the Lord after Ehud died. 2 And the Lord sold them into the hand of Jabin king of Canaan, who reigned in Hazor. The commander of his army was Sisera, who lived in Harosheth-hagoyim. 3 Then the people of Israel cried out to the Lord for help, for he had 900 chariots of iron and he oppressed the people of Israel cruelly for twenty years.* ESV

A3. Why did God allow the Canaanites to treat the Israelites "harshly" for 20 years? (see 4:1)

## BARAK

A4.  Why do you think Deborah went with Barak, rather than insisting he follow God's instructions?
Judges 4:8     *Barak said to her, "If you will go with me, I will go, but if you will not go with me, I will not go."*  ESV

A5.  Deborah said that a woman would win the battle.
Judges 4:9     *And she said, "I will surely go with you. Nevertheless, the road on which you are going will not lead to your glory, for the Lord will sell Sisera into the hand of a woman." Then Deborah arose and went with Barak to Kedesh.*

Q.  What would have been your reaction to this if you were Barak?

A6.  Why do you think Deborah told Barak a woman would win the day?

HEBER

A7.  What was Heber's relationship to the Kenites?
Judges 4:11     *Now Heber the Kenite had separated from the Kenites, the descendants of Hobab the father-in-law of Moses, and had pitched his tent as far away as the oak in Zaanannim, which is near Kedesh.* ESV

A8.  In other translations and commentaries it appears that Heber told Sisera about Barak's battle plans and where he was taking his troops. Why would Heber do this?

B.  JAEL

B1.  Reread 4:18-21. How would you explain the actions of Jael?

B2.  Jael would not have had time to think up a plan in advance because she did not know Sisera was coming. Why do you think Jael invited Sisera into her tent?

B3.  Once Sisera was in the tent Jael probably had some time to think about the consequences of her invitation. If Jael wanted to protect her future, what options did she really have after Sisera was in the tent?

B4.  Do you think Jael's killing of Sisera is a choice she made to correct the mistake of allowing him in her tent, or do you think Jael's loyalties were not with the Canaanites?

B5.  Reread 4:15-16. What did Barak and his army do in the battle?

B6.  What did Sisera, the Canaanite commander, do in the battle?

B7.  Why do you think Sisera went to Jael's tent?

B8.  What cultural norm would make Jael's tent an attractive hiding place for Sisera?

B9.  What was Jael's attitude and demeanor when Sisera arrived?

B10.  Sisera asked for a drink of water. What did Jael give him and why?

B11.  Why do you suppose Jael chose this method of killing Sisera? Would there have been easier methods?

B12.  This incident violated several cultural norms. Where else in Scripture does God elevate women to a role that generally conflicted with the existing culture? Some possibilities might include: Miriam (Ex 15 and Nu 12), Anna (Lk 2:36), and Esther. Can you identify any others?

## C.  SONG OF DEBORAH

C1. How would you describe or characterize Judges Chapter 5?

C2.  How does 5:8 explain 5:6-7?

Judges 5:6-8    *In the days of Shamgar, son of Anath, in the days of Jael, the highways were abandoned, and travelers kept to the byways. 7 The villagers ceased in Israel; they ceased to be until I arose; I, Deborah, arose as a mother in Israel. 8 When new gods were chosen, then war was in the gates. Was shield or spear to be seen among forty thousand in Israel?* ESV

C3.  What does it mean in 5:8 that there were no shields or spears in Israel?

## D.  APPLICATION

D1.  Do you have divided loyalties?

D2.  Who or what are you <u>really</u> loyal to?

D3.  Do you need the courage of Jael for some situation or conflict in your life? Why?

D4.  We see in this story that a number of cultural norms were violated. Are you caught on the web of cultural norms and feel that you must break away from those norms? How could your true friends or your small group assist you?

# *Gomer*
## Hosea's promiscuous wife

---

**Occurrences of "Gomer" in the Bible:** 2

**Themes:** Faithfulness

---

## Scripture

Hosea 1:2-9

*When the Lord first spoke through Hosea, the Lord said to Hosea, "Go, take to yourself a wife of whoredom and have children of whoredom, for the land commits great whoredom by forsaking the Lord." 3 So he went and took Gomer, the daughter of Diblaim, and she conceived and bore him a son.*

*4 And the Lord said to him, "Call his name Jezreel, for in just a little while I will punish the house of Jehu for the blood of Jezreel, and I will put an end to the kingdom of the house of Israel. 5 And on that day I will break the bow of Israel in the Valley of Jezreel."*

*6 She conceived again and bore a daughter. And the Lord said to him, "Call her name No Mercy, for I will no more have mercy on the house of Israel, to forgive them at all. 7 But I will have mercy on the house of Judah, and I will save them by the Lord their God. I will not save them by bow or by sword or by war or by horses or by horsemen."*

*8 When she had weaned No Mercy, she conceived and bore a son. 9 And the Lord said, "Call his name Not My People, for you are not my people, and I am not your God." ESV*

## The Context

Even though Hosea's wife is one of the primary themes in the book of Hosea, her name is actually mentioned only twice and both occur in the first nine verses of the book. The word "wife" referring either to Gomer or Israel appears 7 more times.

The book of Hosea uses the strange story of the prophet Hosea and his promiscuous wife Gomer to describe Israel and her unfaithfulness to Yahweh. Israel had been split into two parts: the Northern Kingdom of Judah and the Southern Kingdom of Israel. King Jeroboam ruled in the North. He had instituted new rules of worship that created a pagan culture in Judah – all political in nature designed to please the people so he could continue to rule. Then Hosea appeared. God used Hosea to send a visual message to Israel through his marriage to the unfaithful Gomer. The marriage was a picture of Israel and her relationship with God.

God told Hosea to marry a promiscuous woman (*whore/harlot*) because the people were acting like harlots in their relationship with Him. Hosea obeyed and married Gomer, who initially remained faithful. Scripture says she "bore him a son." God told Hosea to name the son *Jezreel* ("God scatters" or "God sows").

Gomer bore a second child, but the language used implies that Hosea was probably not the father. That child was to be named *No Compassion*. A third child was born, again without indicating Hosea as the father, and God named this son, *Not My People.*

The mind bending parallel here is that both Hosea and the Lord had unfaithful wives, yet the husbands were faithful. The promiscuous situation and the names of the children were meant to send a loud and clear message to Israel. God wanted Israel to see a physical picture of how the nation was acting. It was God's desire that Hosea's message of condemnation and ultimate hope would get through to the people.

It does not matter whether Gomer was actually working as a prostitute or if she was just a promiscuous woman. Neither does it matter whether this story is an allegory or historical fact. It does not really matter whether Gomer was faithful at first and then later became unfaithful. What does matter is that God showed an unmistakable picture: the Israelites had forsaken their God, were worshipping pagan deities, and had abandoned their moral judgment.

## What Do We Know?

In Hosea 1:2, Hosea was told to marry a woman of *loose morals*:

- a promiscuous wife (Holman)
- an adulterous wife (NIV)
- a wife of whoredom (NRSV)
- a wife of harlotry (NKJV)
- find a whore and marry her (THE MESSAGE)

We get the idea! It is very clear what God asked of Hosea. Israel, God says, is the problem. She has been unfaithful to the Lord. The second verse says, "*for the land commits great whoredom by forsaking the Lord.*" The culture in the land was unfaithfulness. The people had been and were unfaithful. They openly practiced idolatry and worshipped pagan gods. So God told Hosea to marry a promiscuous wife to illustrate Israel's unfaithfulness.

God Himself named the three children. The names called attention to Israel's miserable spiritual condition and were intended to send a clear warning message to Israel. Through Hosea and Gomer's adulterous marriage, God showed a relationship that paralleled His current relationship with Israel. God intended marriage partners to be exclusive (no rivals), just as God Himself wanted no rivals in His position as the God of His people. He was and is a jealous God.

But the illustration does not focus on Gomer alone. Just as God was faithful to His people, so was Hosea faithful to his wife. Hosea did not abandon Gomer. Like a marriage partner, God is involved with the lives of His people, even when they commit idolatry and violate His moral or spiritual code. He will not abandon them. The message for Israel was to stop their idolatry (promiscuous behavior), repent, and return to the Lord their God.

Looking ahead in chapters 2-3 we find the Gospel message:

Israel's Adultery Rebuked:
Hos 2:2    *Plead with your mother, plead—for she is not my wife, and I am not her husband—that she put away her whoring from her face, and her adultery from between her breasts;* ESV

Israel's Lifestyle:
Hos 2:5    *For their mother has played the whore; she who conceived them has acted shamefully. For she said, 'I will go after my lovers, who give me my bread and my water, my wool and my flax, my oil and my drink.'* ESV

The Indictment:
Hos 2:6-13    *Therefore I will hedge up her way with thorns, and I will build a wall against her, so that she cannot find her paths . . . I will take back my grain in its time, and my wine in its season, and I will take away my wool and my flax, which were to cover her nakedness . . . I will put an end to all her mirth, her feasts, her new moons, her Sabbaths, and all her appointed feasts. And I will lay*

*waste her vines and her fig trees . . . I will punish her for the feast days of the Baals . . . ESV*

Restoration – Adultry Forgiven:
Hos 2:14-23     *Therefore, behold, I will allure her, and bring her into the wilderness, and speak tenderly to her. 15 And there I will give her vineyards and make the Valley of Achor a door of hope . . . I will remove the names of the Baals from her mouth, and they shall be remembered by name no more . . . I will make you lie down in safety. 19 And I will betroth you to me forever. I will betroth you to me in righteousness and in justice, in steadfast love and in mercy. 20 I will betroth you to me in faithfulness. And you shall know the Lord . . . I will sow her for myself in the land. And I will have mercy on No Mercy, and I will say to Not My People, 'You are my people'; and he shall say, 'You are my God.' ESV*

Reconciliation:
Hos 3:1, 3     *And the Lord said to me, "Go again, love a woman who is loved by another man and is an adulteress, even as the Lord loves the children of Israel, though they turn to other gods and love cakes of raisins." . . . 3 And I said to her, "You must dwell as mine for many days. You shall not play the whore, or belong to another man; so will I also be to you." ESV*

The Price
Hos 3:2     *So I bought her for fifteen shekels of silver and a homer and a lethech of barley. ESV*


# Implications and Observations


The main character in this story is Gomer. Although it is easy to get caught up in the sensational story about her adulterous life and how Hosea dealt with the situation, the real focus of the story is God and what He wanted to teach Israel. Once we get past

Gomer's adulterous character, there are a number several positive themes in this story:

- Unconditional love.
- Redeeming love.
- Forgiveness.
- Loyalty.
- Faithfulness.

One of the important messages to understand is that Hosea paid the price to redeem Gomer. Yes, Gomer was unfaithful, but Hosea 3:2 tells us that Hosea bought her back. We do not know the exact circumstances that led to her enslavement, but Hosea paid the price to restore Gomer to his family. In spite of all the terrible things that Gomer had done, he redeemed her from her life of sin. Gomer was probably a shell of her former self by that time, but that did not deter Hosea: he paid the cost to restore her to the covenant of marriage to which he had committed.

Does this sound like a story you have heard before? Isn't this the Gospel message? Has not God paid the price with His Son, just as Hosea paid the price for Gomer? And were we not hopelessly lost in a love relationship with the world and with sin when He redeemed us? Restoration is not free. Transgression incurs a debt and justice demands that it be paid.

We often hear that salvation is a free gift, but it is not free. It may be free to you and me, but someone had to pay the cost to make it right with God, You and I owe a legitimate debt that must be paid. Jesus paid that debt for us. He suffered and physically died for us so that our only cost is faith.

In this story Hosea had to buy Gomer back or the entire situation would be absolutely meaningless. If Gomer had not been restored (if Israel had not been redeemed) then the story had no purpose. Gomer's redemption carried a cost, just as the redemption of Israel and ultimately the redemption of all believers has a cost. It was not free.

***Don't be a Gomer!***

# Discussion Questions:

## A.  GENERAL

A1.  Pick one word or phrase as the most important concept in 1:2-9. What would you choose and why?

A2.  2 Kings 17:7-18 tells us why God sent the Northern Kingdom into captivity. What is the reason given in 17:7?

2 Kings 17:7     *And this occurred because the people of Israel had sinned against the Lord their God, who had brought them up out of the land of Egypt from under the hand of Pharaoh king of Egypt, and had feared other gods.* ESV

A3.  In 1:2 we are told why Hosea is given these strange instructions. What is the reason? What does it mean?

Q.  What does this mean about the people?

A4.  How would you have reacted if God had given you a similar command (to marry a harlot)?

A5.  How do you think Hosea was able to deal with the situation?

A6.  If this had been <u>you</u> and you were told to love a promiscuous spouse, how would <u>you</u> have dealt with it? How would you have acted?

A7.  What can you find out about the city of "*Jezreel?*" Why does this city and area fit into this story?  [2 Kings 9 and 10]

A8.  The second child was named *No Compassion*. How does this name fit with the story?

A9.  The third child is named *Not My People*. Why did God use this name?

A10.  How would you explain 2:5b: "*I will go after my lovers, the men who give me my food and water, my wool and flax, my oil and drink.*"

Q.  How does this relate to God's message?

A11.  How does this story compare or contrast to our culture today?

A12.  Why didn't God just give up on Israel?  What should that say to us?

A13.  Why would God restore this adulterous people?

Q.  If there is no faithful remnant, what are God's options?

A14.  What major truths might you suggest this book reveals?

## B.  DIVORCE


B1.  If *Not My People*, is an accurate description, which of the following terms would best and accurately describe the situation?

Divorce?          Abandonment?          Separation?




B2.  Hosea 3:5 indicates that the "divorce" is temporary. How would you interpret 3:4-5?

Hosea 3:4-5    *For the children of Israel shall dwell many days without king or prince, without sacrifice or pillar, without ephod or household gods. 5 Afterward the children of Israel shall return and seek the Lord their God, and David their king, and they shall come in fear to the Lord and to his goodness in the latter days.* ESV


Q.  What "days" or "age" is being described in 3:4?




Q.  Given that King David reigned around 1000 BC and Hosea is prophesied in the 700s BC, who is the author referring to when he says "David their king"?

Q.  Verse 3:5 says "Afterward." After what? When will they come in fear?

B3.  In what way could the word "divorce" be an accurate representation of the situation?

## C.  APPLICATION

C1.  Could anyone charge <u>you</u> with being spiritually promiscuous in any way?

C2.  Have you ever had to rely on God's compassion? Have you ever been concerned that your behavior eliminated you from experiencing God's compassion?

C3.  Are you missing God's warnings? Are you listening but not hearing? Are there prophets today speaking for God and are you (we) ignoring their warnings? Are we dismissing them as misguided eccentrics?

C4.  Have you ever abandoned something or someone and then wanted to return or reconcile? Is there someone in your life with whom reconciliation is needed? How hard would it be? Ask a friend to help.

# *Rizpah*
## King Saul's concubine

---

**Occurrences of "Rizpah" in the Bible:** 4

**Themes:** Faithfulness; Mother's love; Honor

---

## Scripture

2 Samuel 3:1, 6-7　　　Civil War
*There was a long war between the house of Saul and the house of David. And David grew stronger and stronger, while the house of Saul became weaker and weaker. . . . 6 While there was war between the house of Saul and the house of David, Abner was making himself strong in the house of Saul. 7 Now Saul had a concubine whose name was Rizpah, the daughter of Aiah. And Ish-bosheth said to Abner, "Why have you gone in to my father's concubine?" ESV*

2 Sam 21:7-9　　　Justice For the Gibeonites
*But the king spared Mephibosheth, the son of Saul's son Jonathan, because of the oath of the Lord that was between them, between David and Jonathan the son of Saul. 8 The king took the two sons of Rizpah the daughter of Aiah, whom she bore to Saul, Armoni and Mephibosheth; and the five sons of Merab the daughter of Saul, whom she bore to Adriel the son of Barzillai the Meholathite; 9 and he gave them into the hands of the Gibeonites, and they hanged*

*them on the mountain before the Lord, and the seven of them perished together. They were put to death in the first days of harvest, at the beginning of barley harvest. ESV*

## 2 Sam 21:10-14    Rizpah Mourns the Dead

*Then Rizpah the daughter of Aiah took sackcloth and spread it for herself on the rock, from the beginning of harvest until rain fell upon them from the heavens. And she did not allow the birds of the air to come upon them by day, or the beasts of the field by night. 11 When David was told what Rizpah the daughter of Aiah, the concubine of Saul, had done, 12 David went and took the bones of Saul and the bones of his son Jonathan from the men of Jabesh-gilead, who had stolen them from the public square of Beth-shan, where the Philistines had hanged them, on the day the Philistines killed Saul on Gilboa. 13 And he brought up from there the bones of Saul and the bones of his son Jonathan; and they gathered the bones of those who were hanged. 14 And they buried the bones of Saul and his son Jonathan in the land of Benjamin in Zela, in the tomb of Kish his father. And they did all that the king commanded. And after that God responded to the plea for the land. ESV*

# The Context:

In 2 Samuel 3 Saul's son Ish-bosheth questioned Abner (one of King Saul's generals), about why he had slept with Rizpah, Saul's concubine. The text never says whether or not Abner actually slept with Rizpah but Abner became angry and indignant at the accusation. He felt his loyalty was being questioned, and even asked God to punish him if he was guilty. Abner defected to David but was later assassinated by Joab. Joab, who was loyal to King Saul, killed Abner by stabbing him in the stomach, just as Abner had killed Joab's brother during the battle at Gibeon. It is important to recognize that Abner killed Joab's brother in battle, but Joab killed Abner in peacetime.

Rizpah's name appears in Scripture again in 2 Samuel 21. She bore King Saul two sons named Armoni and Mephibosheth, who were among the men David handed over to the Gibeonites in retribution for past bloodshed by Saul. The Gibeonites had agreed to be satisfied if David would turn over to them seven members of Saul's family for public execution in Saul's hometown of Gibeah.

The men were executed and Rizpah, the mother of two of the seven, performed an act of love and compassion by watching over the remains of the bodies. In response David gathered the bones of Saul and his family and honored them by burying them in the tomb of Saul's father, Kish.

The text says that following this, "God answered prayer for the land."

## What Do We Know?

While the text does not specifically say that Rizpah was Saul's former concubine, we can be reasonably sure that she was. If we are examining only Rizpah and what she did for her sons, her past history with Saul and Abner does not really impact the story, but it is part of the overall picture. Unfortunately, the two sons Rizpah bore to Saul became collateral damage in the war between Saul and David.

In 2 Sam 21:1 the Lord identified King Saul's past bloodshed of the Gibeonites as the reason for the famine that was occurring at that time. God did not tell David how to fix the problem, but David's actions in recognizing and easing the Gibeonite's pain were apparently adequate to satisfy the Lord because after this, "God answered prayer for the land."

The real story here is Rizpah and her love and loyalty to her family, particularly her two dead sons. Rizpah's actions were driven by her love for her sons and not because of any relationship with either King Saul or Abner, who were both now dead. Rizpah performed an act of honor and respect for both her sons as well as the five others who were killed. In reality this would have been a 24/7 commitment as she had to protect the bodies from both the hot sun and the birds during the day and from wild animals at night. This probably meant that there was not much time for her to do anything else, including sleep.

## Implications and Observations

Based on what is known about the harvests in Israel, most commentators believe that the bodies were left exposed to the elements for as long as five months. Whatever the exact time, the fact remains that Rizpah performed this act of honor and love for an extended period. Her actions were enough to attract David's attention and remind him that Saul's remains had been treated inappropriately. So, probably with some feeling of guilt, David collected the remains of Saul and his son Jonathan and buried them in a place that would honor the former king and his family.

- The focus of this story is what Rizpah did. It is reported in just two verses: she spread her mourning clothes (sackcloth) on a rock for a place to sit and to watch.
- She was there from the beginning of the barley harvest (March-April?) until the rains came (probably October).
- She did not allow the birds during the day or wild animals at night to disturb the bodies.

NOTE: It is possible that the length of time Rizpah guarded the bodies was only 6-10 weeks, if the reference to rain is the spring rains.

It would have been extremely distressing for Rizpah to look upon her sons' rotting bodies. A woman of lesser strength and inner fortitude would have never considered such an act and even if she did she would have soon melted in the heat of the day or been frightened away at the first howl in the night.

## Discussion Questions

### A.  GENERAL

A1.  What are the facts and circumstances of Rizpah's life as reported in 2 Samuel 3:1-16?

    a)   Rizpah was a _____ from Saul's harem.

    b)   Saul was dead and his son Ish-bosheth was now the head or leader of the house of _____.

    c)   Ish-bosheth accused Abner of sleeping with _____.

    d)   Abner was furious and claimed he did not sleep with _____.

A2.  Abner's position and strength had been growing in the house of Saul. Then Saul's son who headed up a local government, accused Abner of sleeping with the concubine Rizpah. Why would Abner have been questioned about his reason for sleeping with one of Saul's concubines (3:7)?

A3.  Do we know whether Abner actually slept with Rizpah?

A4.  How did this accusation against Abner and Rizpah impact Abner's relationship with Ish-bosheth?

A5.  Why do you think the story about Rizpah and Abner is included in the Bible? What does it allow us to learn? (review 3:1-16)

DAVID/SAUL

ISRAEL

SIX SONS

MICHAL

A6.  What were the circumstances surrounding Rizpah's life as reported in 2 Samuel 21:1-14?

a)  During this time there was a famine in the land for
_____ successive years.

b)  The Lord told David that the famine was the result of the bloodshed Saul instigated against the
_____, breaking an _____ of peace.

c)  David asked the Gibeonites how the situation could be resolved and they required that they be given seven of
_____ male descendants to execute in Gibeah.

d)  David agreed and two of the people executed were sons of _____.

e)  _____began a round-the-clock vigil to protect the bodies from birds and animals.

f) Ultimately David retrieved the bones of Saul, Jonathan, and the seven executed at Gibeah and buried them in the tomb of _____ (Saul's father).


g) After that the Lord answered prayer for the _____.


A7. How do we know for sure that the Rizpah in chapter 21 was the concubine identified in 2 Samuel 3?


A8. Read carefully 2 Sam 21:7-8. Are there one or two people named Mephibosheth? Was Mephibosheth (Rizpah's son) killed or not?


## B. BACKGROUND


King Saul had previously broken the Israelite oath with the Gibeonites which resulted in three years of drought:
2 Samuel 21:1   *Now there was a famine in the days of David for three years, year after year. And David sought the face of the Lord. And the Lord said, "There is bloodguilt on Saul and on his house, because he put the Gibeonites to death."* ESV

For some unknown reason, King Saul had attempted to annihilate the Gibeonites even though Israel had sworn an oath to spare them. David, in an attempt to bring closure and peace with the Gibeonites asked how he could make amends. They demanded seven of Saul's male descendants be executed in the public square of Saul's home town. David agreed and Mephibosheth, Jonathon's son was not chosen, but a son by the same name born to Rizpah and King Saul was one of the seven executed!

B1.  No one collected bodies from the fields of war. Corpses simply decomposed there or were carried away by animals. Why would Rizpah have been unwilling to allow this to happen?

B2.  Rizpah's act was certainly a heartfelt response to a terrible situation. How might you argue that:

(a)  It was not necessary or worth it.

(b) It was worth it.

## C.  RIZPAH

C1.  Why do you think Rizpah did this?

C2.  Rizpah was a former concubine of King Saul. Given this fact, what would she have been like? What sort of life would she have led (excluding her sexual responsibilities)?

> Q.  How do you harmonize Rizpah's probable nature and physical attributes with her ability to undertake this ritual for her sons?

C3.  What protection did Rizpah have from the elements?

> Q.  Geographically, where were these bodies on display?

C4.  Why would Rizpah choose a rock on which to watch and sleep?

C5.  Why wouldn't she have removed the bodies to a safe place of burial?

C6.  Why wouldn't she have gotten help to watch and protect?

C7.  If you were Rizpah during this time of guarding the bodies, what would you have been thinking?

C8.  What ended the drama of protecting the bodies (see 2 Sam 21:13-14)?

C9.  Based on 2 Sam 21:13, was Rizpah's ordeal in vain?

C10.  Rizpah's act obviously prompted David to honor the remains of Saul and Jonathan. What impact would the drama have had on people in the area who observed the scene?

C11.  After it was all over, how might Rizpah have been impacted by the ordeal?

## D.  APPLICATION

D1.  Do you have a family member who has been overlooked and should be honored in some way?

D2.  Do you need to go to a family member and correct some kind of disrespect that they are shouldering?

D3.  How would you compare your love for your family to that exhibited by Rizpah?

D4.  Is there anything in your life today that requires you setting aside all other responsibilities and giving it your full attention?

D5.  This is a dramatic story about a mother's love. What other emotion or feeling would you think might compare with a mother's love? Have you ever experienced anything similar to what we see in Rizpah's life?

# *Woman of Tekoa*
## who pretended to mourn

---

**Occurrences of "woman of Tekoa" in the Bible:** 3
Five additional times she is referred to
simply as "the woman."

**Themes:** Trickery; Discernment

---

## Scripture

2 Samuel 14:1-24, 28-33

Absalom Restored to David

*Now Joab the son of Zeruiah knew that the king's heart went out to Absalom. 2 And Joab sent to Tekoa and brought from there a wise woman and said to her, "Pretend to be a mourner and put on mourning garments. Do not anoint yourself with oil, but behave like a woman who has been mourning many days for the dead. 3 Go to the king and speak thus to him." So Joab put the words in her mouth.*

*4 When the woman of Tekoa came to the king, she fell on her face to the ground and paid homage and said, "Save me, O king." 5 And the king said to her, "What is your trouble?" She answered, "Alas, I am a widow; my husband is dead. 6 And your servant had two sons, and they quarreled with one another in the field. There was no one to separate them, and one struck the other and killed him. 7 And now the whole clan has risen against your servant, and they say, 'Give up the man who struck his brother, that we may put him to death for the life of his brother whom he killed.' And so they would destroy the heir also. Thus they would quench my coal that is left and leave to my husband neither name nor remnant on the face of the earth."*

8 Then the king said to the woman, "Go to your house, and I will give orders concerning you." 9 And the woman of Tekoa said to the king, "On me be the guilt, my lord the king, and on my father's house; let the king and his throne be guiltless." 10 The king said, "If anyone says anything to you, bring him to me, and he shall never touch you again." 11 Then she said, "Please let the king invoke the Lord your God, that the avenger of blood kill no more, and my son be not destroyed." He said, "As the Lord lives, not one hair of your son shall fall to the ground."

12 Then the woman said, "Please let your servant speak a word to my lord the king." He said, "Speak." 13 And the woman said, "Why then have you planned such a thing against the people of God? For in giving this decision the king convicts himself, inasmuch as the king does not bring his banished one home again. 14 We must all die; we are like water spilled on the ground, which cannot be gathered up again. But God will not take away life, and he devises means so that the banished one will not remain an outcast. 15 Now I have come to say this to my lord the king because the people have made me afraid, and your servant thought, 'I will speak to the king; it may be that the king will perform the request of his servant. 16 For the king will hear and deliver his servant from the hand of the man who would destroy me and my son together from the heritage of God.' 17 And your servant thought, 'The word of my lord the king will set me at rest,' for my lord the king is like the angel of God to discern good and evil. The Lord your God be with you!"

18 Then the king answered the woman, "Do not hide from me anything I ask you." And the woman said, "Let my lord the king speak." 19 The king said, "Is the hand of Joab with you in all this?" The woman answered and said, "As surely as you live, my lord the king, one cannot turn to the right hand or to the left from anything that my lord the king has said. It was your servant Joab who commanded me; it was he who put all these words in the mouth of your servant. 20 In order to change the course of things your servant Joab did this. But my lord has wisdom like the wisdom of the angel of God to know all things that are on the earth."
21 Then the king said to Joab, "Behold now, I grant this; go, bring back the young man Absalom." 22 And Joab fell on his face to the ground and paid homage and blessed the king. And Joab said,

*"Today your servant knows that I have found favor in your sight, my lord the king, in that the king has granted the request of his servant." 23 So Joab arose and went to Geshur and brought Absalom to Jerusalem. 24 And the king said, "Let him dwell apart in his own house; he is not to come into my presence." So Absalom lived apart in his own house and did not come into the king's presence. . . .*

*28 So Absalom lived two full years in Jerusalem, without coming into the king's presence. 29 Then Absalom sent for Joab, to send him to the king, but Joab would not come to him. And he sent a second time, but Joab would not come. 30 Then he said to his servants, "See, Joab's field is next to mine, and he has barley there; go and set it on fire." So Absalom's servants set the field on fire.*

*31 Then Joab arose and went to Absalom at his house and said to him, "Why have your servants set my field on fire?" 32 Absalom answered Joab, "Behold, I sent word to you, 'Come here, that I may send you to the king, to ask, "Why have I come from Geshur? It would be better for me to be there still." Now therefore let me go into the presence of the king, and if there is guilt in me, let him put me to death.'" 33 Then Joab went to the king and told him, and he summoned Absalom. So he came to the king and bowed himself on his face to the ground before the king, and the king kissed Absalom.* ESV

## The Context

This story in Chapter 14 is about the restoration of Absalom to his father King David after Absalom had killed his brother Amnon, David's oldest son, because Amnon had raped Tamar. Tamar was David's daughter by Maacah (see 2 Sam 3:3). She was Absalom's full sister, and a virgin when Amnon raped her.

Amnon had pretended to be sick and convinced David to send Tamar to him to prepare food for him. Amnon ordered all the servants out of the house and raped Tamar. He then refused to ask David for permission to marry her and expelled her from his house.

Her brother Absalom took her into his house where she lived a desolate life.

> 2 Samuel 13:21-22    *When King David heard of all these things, he was very angry. 22 But Absalom spoke to Amnon neither good nor bad, for Absalom hated Amnon, because he had violated his sister Tamar.* ESV

Two years later Absalom invited his father David to come to a sheep shearing "party." David declined but Absalom convinced him to send all his other sons, including Amnon. Absalom ordered his men to kill Amnon after he was high from drinking wine. The king's other sons escaped and Absalom fled to avoid his father's wrath.

> 2 Samuel 13:38-39    *So Absalom fled and went to Geshur, and was there three years. 39 And the spirit of the king longed to go out to Absalom, because he was comforted about Amnon, since he was dead.* ESV

## What Do We Know?

Chapter 13 ends with the statement that, "David had finished grieving over Amnon's death," but this is in conflict with chapter 14. Verse 13:39 says that King David longed to see Absalom but that is contradicted by the king's actions in chapter 14.

Absalom was staying with his grandfather in Geshur, a small city-state on the eastern side of the Sea of Galilee. It would have been a relatively easy trip for David to visit his son if he really wanted to see him. Or the king could simply have asked Absalom to visit him in Jerusalem. Neither of these things happened. We do not know the exact reasons for the continuing separation given that the text says David "longed to go to Absalom."

Joab seems to have recognized that even though David had finished grieving for Amnon, he was not strong enough to reach out to his son. It is likely that although his active grieving was over, David's feelings toward Absalom were still very raw and he determined that it was best to delay meeting. It is also possible that although the grieving was over and he really wanted to see Absalom, he was still angry over the entire situation and was afraid of how he might react upon seeing Absalom face-to-face.

Joab may have been wise enough to perceive all this so he devised a plan to force the king to recognize how his feelings were impacting his actions. Thus enters the woman from Tekoa.

Joab began by concocting a story involving a "wise woman" from Tekoa, a small town south of Jerusalem. Joab instructed the woman to go to King David with the following story:

- I am a widow.
- I had two sons and one killed the other.
- The family has demanded the living son be put to death.
- This means the family will have no heir and no son to carry on the family name.

David responded to the story by telling the woman to go home and he would issue an order on her behalf. The woman then asked that any blame for such order rest on her and her father's family and not on the king. The woman requested that David reaffirm his order, probably with an oath, that her son should not be harmed, and the king responded, "*As the Lord lives, not one hair of your son shall fall to the ground.*"

At that point the woman applied the story to King David and his relationship with his son Absalom, implying that the people of

Israel wanted their prince reinstated in the king's good graces.

David rightly discerned that Joab was behind the fabricated story but decided to relent. He told Joab to go to Absalom and bring him back to Jerusalem. But David ordered that when he returned, Absalom should go to his own house and not see his father. After two years the king finally relented from his separation order and allowed Absalom to return to the presence of the king.

## Discussion Questions

### A.  GENERAL

A1.  How do you think that Joab observed or discerned that David's mind was on Absalom?

A2.  Why do you think that Joab sent for a woman from Tekoa? There were certainly clever women in Jerusalem.

A3.  The text says that Joab sought a wise or clever woman. What other characteristics might have been of equal importance?

A4.  Do you imagine it was easy finding a woman who fit the requirements and was willing?

Q.  Why would someone accept the assignment?

A5.  If you were the woman and had been approached under these circumstances, would you have accepted the assignment? Why? Why not?

A6.  Why did the king order protection for the woman's living son?

A7.　How would you explain that David made little attempt to understand all the issues?

A8.　The king gave the woman what she asked for. Why did she continue to press the matter? (14:9-11)

A9.　On what basis would the woman say: *"On me be the guilt, my lord the king, and on my father's house; let the king and his throne be guiltless."* (2 Samuel 14:9) Is this not a significant risk for a woman who is only an actor in a scheme?

　　Q.　Do you think this was part of the original instruction from Joab, or did she say it in the excitement of the moment?

A10.　If you had been the king, what would have been your immediate reaction to this story?

A11.  What clever thing did the woman say in the first sentence of 14:13 that might have appealed to David?

A12.  What did the woman do in 14:15-16 and why?

A13.  Who was 14:17 aimed at?

2 Samuel 14:17      *And your servant thought, 'The word of my lord the king will set me at rest,' for my lord the king is like the angel of God to discern good and evil. The Lord your God be with you!"* ESV

Q.  How does it describe the king?

A14.  What did the king do as a result of the woman's role-playing and why?

## B. JOAB

B1.  What do we know about Joab?

B2.  What did the woman do or say in 14:19-20 after David asked if Joab had instigated this scheme?

Acknowledged David as _____, whom no one can disobey.

Readily admitted that _____ was the mastermind of the scheme.

Blamed _____ for everything she had said.

Declared the king to be wise and discerning like the angel of God, knowing _____ on earth.

B3.  At the king's request Joab brought Absalom to Jerusalem. But there was a catch! What was it?

B4.  Why do you suppose David did this? What was he thinking?

## C.  DISCERNMENT

DEFINITION of discernment: to detect; to recognize or identify; to understand the difference; the ability to grasp and comprehend what is obscure; the ability to perceive the facts and understand. (Webster)

C1.  Following are examples of discernment and lack of discernment in this story. Some may simply be decisions, but for this purpose let's consider them all discernment. Identify which discernments were accurate and which were inaccurate.

14:1 _____ Joab discerned that king's mind was on Absalom.

14:8 _____ David agreed to issue a command on her behalf (confirmed again in 14:11). He failed to discern that this was a fabricated story.

14:19 _____ He sensed Joab's hand in the situation.

14:21 _____ He ordered Absalom's return.


14:24 _____ He allowed Absalom to return to the city but not to David's presence.


14:29 _____ Absalom sent for Joab, but Joab refused to come.


14:31 _____ Joab asked Absalom why his servants set fire to Joab's field.

4:33 _____ David summoned Absalom, who came and bowed down with his face to the ground before the king. Then the king kissed Absalom.


C2. What did the king gain by his decision to allow Absalom to return to his house, but not see him?




C3. What do we learn about discernment from this story?



Q. What does this tell you about the skill of discernment?

C4.  What actions would likely improve one's ability to accurately discern and understand challenging situations?

a)  Take _____ to think. Do not rush to conclusions.

b)  Think about the cause and effect. What consequences will my _____ create or cause?

c)  Ask questions to obtain information and _____ .

d)  Confirm _____ and _____ .

e)  Ask for advice and opinions from trusted _____ .

NOTE:  Many people who are credited with having great discernment actually have only common or average abilities, but they approach questions and situations in an organized manner and think them through logically. Many of us simply do not take the time to think!

## D.  APPLICATION

D1.  Do you need to improve your discernment? Why?

D2.  In what part of your life is discernment needed?

D3.  Is there anything in your life that you need to perceive clearly? Is there something you are refusing to see?

D4.  Do you know you need to reconcile or forgive somebody but you are just letting it slide?

# *Tabitha (Dorcus)*
## Peter raised her from the dead

---

**Occurrences of "Tabitha/Dorcus" in the Bible:** 2/2

**Themes:** Miracles; Death

---

## Scripture

Acts 9:36-42    Tabitha/Dorcas Restored to Life

*Now there was in Joppa a disciple named Tabitha, which, translated, means Dorcas. She was full of good works and acts of charity. 37 In those days she became ill and died, and when they had washed her, they laid her in an upper room. 38 Since Lydda was near Joppa, the disciples, hearing that Peter was there, sent two men to him, urging him, "Please come to us without delay." 39 So Peter rose and went with them. And when he arrived, they took him to the upper room. All the widows stood beside him weeping and showing tunics and other garments that Dorcas made while she was with them. 40 But Peter put them all outside, and knelt down and prayed; and turning to the body he said, "Tabitha, arise." And she opened her eyes, and when she saw Peter she sat up. 41 And he gave her his hand and raised her up. Then calling the saints and widows, he presented her alive. 42 And it became known throughout all Joppa, and many believed in the Lord. 43 And he stayed in Joppa for many days with one Simon, a tanner. ESV*

## The Context:

In the four verses prior to Acts 9:36, Peter was in Lydda where he had healed a paralytic named Aeneas. The impact on the community had been significant: we are told that all who lived there saw the man who was healed and turned toward God. It would be logical to assume that news of this healing miracle had reached the believing community in Joppa.

Joppa was a seaport city on the Mediterranean Sea about 40 miles northwest of Jerusalem, and Lydda was between Joppa and Jerusalem, about 12 miles away. The name of the city eventually became "Jaffa" and it is a suburb of Tel Aviv today.

## What Do We Know?

There is no reason to believe that Tabitha was not really dead. The disciples washed the body and began burial preparations so her death should not be in question. We are not told why the body was not completely prepared for burial. Bodies were typically buried within 24 hours due to the desert-like heat.

The text does not say what the disciples did or said that caused Peter to leave Lydda and go immediately to Joppa. It is very possible that complete healing was in mind because he did not delay. The text implies he left immediately upon hearing the news about Tabitha.

We are told that Tabitha did good works. The text suggests that at least a portion of her good works and charity were directed toward widows. The widows were such good friends and so appreciative that they brought samples of what Tabitha had given them over the years to the house to show other visitors.

Peter knelt and asked God to perform a miracle and bring life back into Tabitha. Peter sent the widows and most visitors out of the room. Family members and some disciples may have been present.

The ones who were or were not present are not important in this story. What is important is Peter's prayer and God's response. The result on the community was the same as in Lydda when Peter healed Aeneas: it became known throughout all the town of Joppa, and many people believed in the Lord.

## Implications and Observations

We know it's highly likely that the disciples in Joppa had heard about Peter healing Aeneas in Lydda. We can logically assume they wanted Peter to come and heal Tabitha. Since Peter did not know Tabitha, there was no obvious reason for Peter to come to a wake. Given the fact that the family did not prepare the body for burial, we might reasonably assume their request was in hopes he would raise Tabitha from death. The fact that Peter came immediately lends support for the position that he came with that thought in mind.

Why would God choose to honor Peter's request for a miracle? We have no reason to believe that Tabitha was important to any other plans the Lord wanted her to complete. Thus, the obvious reason is the positive impact such a healing would have on both believers and non-believers in the area.

It is interesting to note that, other than Jesus, the New Testament records that five people were raised from the dead – none famous or influential. They were all just regular people without any special following.

## Discussion Questions

### A.  MIRACLES

A1.  What is a miracle? How would you define a miracle?

A2.  What other Biblical words are used to describe supernatural events other than "miracle?"

A3.  Who or what do you think of when you hear about a miracle?

A4.  Are you suspicious of reported "miracles"? Why? Why not? Should you be?

A5.  In general, why did Jesus perform miracles? Why did He give power to the Apostles to do miracles? What do you think are the purposes of miracles?

A6.  Given there are true, valid and even obvious miracles today, why do you think some people:
> 1) refuse to believe the miracle, or
> 2) want complete, full, and technical explanation of what happened?

A7.  Have you ever experienced a healing miracle or significant transformation in your life or in the life of someone you know?

HEALING: _____

_____

TRANSFORMATION: _____

_____

A8.  Do you think miracles like Tabitha happen in the same way today? Explain.

A9.  Why do you think both Jesus (raising Jairus daughter – Mk 5:22) and Peter sent people out of the room before their miracle?

## B.  TABITHA

B1.  Why do you think Tabitha was raised and brought back to life, but Stephen (Acts 8:54-60) was killed and not raised? Stephen seems more important to the cause of Christ than Tabitha! Why Tabitha and not Stephen?

B2.  What do you imagine or think Tabitha was doing when the text says she was "doing works and acts of charity"?

B3.  What do you see as the most important fact, concept, or occurrence in this story?  Why?

B4.  Why "come at once" or "don't delay in coming"?

B5.  Why do you suppose they put Tabitha in an upstairs room and did not bury her?

B6.  How do you think the men who went to Lydda to get Peter convinced him to come to Joppa immediately?

B7.  The Bible does not report Peter raising anyone from the dead prior to this time. What do you imagine Peter was thinking or doing while he was walking to Joppa (12 miles)?

B8.  What are the possibilities if Peter prayed publically to raise Tabitha from the dead and it did not happen?

B9.  How would you have reacted to this event if you had been in the house when Peter brought Tabitha downstairs alive?

## C.  RAISED FROM DEAD

C1.  Was Tabitha "resurrected" or raised from the dead?  What is the difference?

C2.  The Old Testament reports three people were raised from the dead. Who were they?

C3.  The New Testament gives reports of five people being raised from the dead. Who were they>

## D.  APPLICATION

D1.  Do you need a miracle in your life? Have you seriously asked for it?

D2.  Do you know someone else who needs a miracle?

D3.  Who are you praying for that needs a miracle?

D4.  What are the things that get in <u>your</u> way of responding to the needs of others?

D5.  Does your life and ministry point people to Jesus or to self?

# The Other Mary
## mother of James

---

**Occurrences of "other Mary" or "mother of James"
in the Bible: 2/4**

**Themes:** Sabbath

**Sabbath**: the practice of observing one day in seven
as a time for rest and worship.

---

## Scripture

Mark 15:39-41

*And when the centurion, who stood facing him, saw that in this way
he breathed his last, he said, "Truly this man was the Son of God!"
40 There were also women looking on from a distance, among
whom were Mary Magdalene, and Mary the mother of James the
younger and of Joses, and Salome. 41 When he was in Galilee, they
followed him and ministered to him, and there were also many
other women who came up with him to Jerusalem.* ESV

Matt 27:59-61

*And Joseph took the body and wrapped it in a clean linen shroud 60
and laid it in his own new tomb, which he had cut in the rock. And
he rolled a great stone to the entrance of the tomb and went away.
61 Mary Magdalene and the other Mary were there, sitting
opposite the tomb.* ESV

Luke 23:54-56

*It was the day of Preparation, and the Sabbath was beginning. 55
The women who had come with him from Galilee followed and saw*

the tomb and how his body was laid. 56 Then they returned and prepared spices and ointments. On the Sabbath they rested according to the commandment. ESV

## Matt 28:1-2
Now after the Sabbath, toward the dawn of the first day of the week, Mary Magdalene and the other Mary went to see the tomb. 2 And behold, there was a great earthquake, for an angel of the Lord descended from heaven and came and rolled back the stone and sat on it. ESV

## Matt 12:1-12
At that time Jesus went through the grain fields on the Sabbath. His disciples were hungry, and they began to pluck heads of grain and to eat. 2 But when the Pharisees saw it, they said to him, "Look, your disciples are doing what is not lawful to do on the Sabbath." 3 He said to them, "Have you not read what David did when he was hungry, and those who were with him: 4 how he entered the house of God and ate the bread of the Presence, which it was not lawful for him to eat nor for those who were with him, but only for the priests? 5 Or have you not read in the Law how on the Sabbath the priests in the temple profane the Sabbath and are guiltless? 6 I tell you, something greater than the temple is here. 7 And if you had known what this means, 'I desire mercy, and not sacrifice,' you would not have condemned the guiltless. 8 For the Son of Man is lord of the Sabbath."

## A Man with a Withered Hand
9 He went on from there and entered their synagogue. 10 And a man was there with a withered hand. And they asked him, "Is it lawful to heal on the Sabbath?"—so that they might accuse him. 11 He said to them, "Which one of you who has a sheep, if it falls into a pit on the Sabbath, will not take hold of it and lift it out? 12 Of how much more value is a man than a sheep! So it is lawful to do good on the Sabbath." ESV

# The Context

A close study of all the gospels reveals that the mother of James was listed as one of the women present at Jesus' crucifixion as well as when His body was laid in the tomb. In addition, she was one of the women who found the tomb empty. She is referred to by several names, including "the other Mary." I believe the multiple names and reference as the "other Mary" was to distinguish her from Mary Magdalene, who had a leading role in the band of women caring for Jesus during His ministry and helping with His burial.

The focus for this study is not Mary herself but the Sabbath. She and the group of women helpers and benefactors could not adequately prepare Christ's body because of the Sabbath. They could not "work" on the Sabbath because it was the day of rest, and working would have violated the Jewish laws. Matthew 27 reports that some of the preparation was done but the work had to be halted because the Sabbath was about to begin. Therefore, the women went back to their homes, or wherever they were staying, and prepared additional spices and perfumes for the first day after the Sabbath when they could go back and finish the work.

The Sabbath was a fundamental part of the Jewish Law. Each part of the law given to Moses at Mt. Sinai contained sections dealing with the Sabbath. Thus, the Ten Commandments, the civil law, and the ceremonial laws all have rules regarding observing the Sabbath. Keeping the Sabbath proclaimed to the world that God ruled in Israel. Breaking the Sabbath was a serious offense, punishable by death (Ex. 31:14).

The Jewish leaders were so concerned about keeping the Sabbath holy and acceptable to God that they developed a large volume of rules and regulations for the people to ensure proper compliance. Supposedly, following all the rules would keep them from violating God's intent for the Sabbath. Ultimately this resulted in substituting man's law for God's law (Mt 15:9), and the rules became a burden rather than a help. The result was that the Sabbath lost its meaning and rather than impacting man's heart and soul, it became nothing more than an outward observance (Mt 12:8) – like repeating a prayer or creed every Sunday becomes automatic to the point of losing meaning.

## What Do We Know?

The Fourth Commandment established the Sabbath:

> Exodus 20:8-11     *"Remember the Sabbath day, to keep it holy. 9 Six days you shall labor, and do all your work, 10 but the seventh day is a Sabbath to the Lord your God. On it you shall not do any work, you, or your son, or your daughter, your male servant, or your female servant, or your livestock, or the sojourner who is within your gates. 11 For in six days the Lord made heaven and earth, the sea, and all that is in them, and rested the seventh day. Therefore the Lord blessed the Sabbath day and made it holy.* ESV

Luke 23:54 says it was "Preparation day," and the Sabbath was about to begin. "Preparation day" was the day before the Sabbath or before any other religious celebration. It was always on a Friday, the day before the Saturday Sabbath, because all festivals began on the Sabbath.

One might wonder why these Christ-followers were keeping the Jewish laws and were so concerned about not working when Jesus' body was only partially prepared for burial and lying in a tomb. Remember, the Christian practice of worshipping on the first day of the week had not yet begun and Jesus Himself had honored the Jewish traditions. It would have been natural to follow and obey the existing practices honoring the Sabbath:

> Lev 23:3   *"Six days shall work be done, but on the seventh day is a Sabbath of solemn rest, a holy convocation. You shall do no work. It is a Sabbath to the Lord in all your dwelling places.* ESV

This Commandment sets apart the seventh day as God's day, reserved for a Sabbath. God set the pattern Himself by resting from His labor of creating the world and all that is in it. "Sabbath" means rest, but God intended for this day to consist of more than simply and absence of work. God's Sabbath is intended to be a day of rest, holy worship, and a drawing near to Him. In effect, God is saying that we have enough time for ourselves in six days; the seventh day is reserved for Him.

By observing the Sabbath, Israel declared that they worshipped Yahweh, the Creator God who made the world. This distinguished them from all other nations who worshipped false gods which they themselves made.

God was very clear about what it meant to observe the Sabbath:

- **when** – seventh day, after six days' of labor.
- **why** – (1) as a day of rest, (2) as a holy day, and (3) set apart to God.
- **who** – the entire family, servants, even including "aliens."
- **how** – think of it in advance, keep it holy, and observe the requirements.

## Implications and Observations

The Sabbath was first established at Sinai when God gave Moses the Ten Commandments and the Law, and it was also confirmed when Israel entered Canaan (Dt 5:12-15). The prohibition of working on the Sabbath seems absolute, but works of necessity or compassion were within the spirit and intent of the commandment. (Mt 12:12; Luke 14:5). The New Testament identifies several exceptions to the Sabbath Law:

> Works of mercy
> Mt 12:12    *Of how much more value is a man than a sheep! So it is lawful to do good on the Sabbath.* ESV

> Necessities
> Luke 13:15-16    *Then the Lord answered him, "You hypocrites! Does not each of you on the Sabbath untie his ox or his donkey from the manger and lead it away to water it? 16 And ought not this woman, a daughter of Abraham whom Satan bound for eighteen years, be loosed from this bond on the Sabbath day?"* ESV

God did not stop all work. He continued sustaining, maintaining, and redeeming the world on the Sabbath. He did cease from creating, shaping, and forming it. That is the nature of what God wants men to cease as well, and to focus their attention on Him. We are to set the day apart for Him! He wants us to stop thinking about work, hobbies, family, and friends. We are to cast our anxieties on Him, worship Him, and focus our attention on Him. He wants us to continue our routines on the other six days of the week. Grasping that concept is not hard. What is hard is unwrapping ourselves from the world that wants to ignore God.

Observing the Sabbath seems like a very clear example of where the world has influenced the church rather than the church influencing the world. Even for many believers, observing the Sabbath often involves little more than setting aside an hour or two for church attendance.

*Keep the Sabbath holy!*

# Discussion Questions

## A. JEWISH SABBATH

A1.  What was the Sabbath?
SUGGESTION: Answer this before answering any of the following questions. After you have completed all the discussion questions, come back and see if you want to change your answer here.

A2. What was the purpose of the Sabbath? From study notes or a commentary see if you can locate a good succinct description for the <u>purpose</u> of the Sabbath.

A3.  What is the basic difference between the Old Testament Sabbath and the New Testament Sunday Worship service?

A4.  Based on Ex 31:13-16 God takes the Sabbath seriously:
*Say to the Israelites, You must observe my Sabbaths. This will be a sign between me and you for the generations to come, so you may know that I am the LORD, who makes you holy. 14 Observe the Sabbath, because it is holy to you. <u>Anyone who desecrates it must be put to death</u>; whoever does any work on that day must be cut off from his people . . . celebrating it for the generations to come as a lasting covenant.* NIV

> Q.  What is meant or implied when God says to observe, <u>My</u> Sabbaths?

> Q.  Who or what is God making holy?

> Q.  Who is to make the Sabbath holy?

> Q.  What exactly does this say is the purpose of the Sabbath?

A5.  What does it mean in Ex 31:13 that this day is described as a "sign"?

A6.  What do you think it means that the Sabbath was to be kept holy?




A7. What is the significance or what does it mean that the Sabbath was "*to the Lord*" (Ex 20:10)?
Exodus 20:10    *but the seventh day is a Sabbath <u>to the Lord</u> your God. You shall not do any work . . .* ESV




A8.  What did it mean that the Sabbath was to be a "day of sacred assembly"?
Leviticus 23:3    *For six days work may be done, but on the seventh day there must be a Sabbath of complete rest, a sacred assembly. You are not to do any work; it is a Sabbath to the Lord wherever you live.*




## B.  SUNDAY WORSHIP

B1.  The Bible says in Ex 31:16-17 that Israel was a covenant people. They were chosen, called, and made holy (separated from the world). The Sabbath was a sign of this relationship. Do you think of yourself in similar terms? Today, is Sunday a <u>very special</u> day for you or is it more like all the other days of the week? Why? Why not?

B2.  The Jewish Sabbath was instituted by God for the Jewish people. Who and what do you think Sunday is for today?

WHO:  _____

WHAT:  _____

B3.  Do <u>you</u> think or treat Sunday as "holy" today? Why? Why not?

Q. Assuming it should be kept holy, what type of activities <u>should</u> we do (or not do) to make Sunday holy?

DO:  _____.

_____.

NOT DO: _____.

Q.  What do we <u>actually</u> do on Sunday?

B4.  In what ways do <u>you</u> think God is being dishonored today on Sunday?

B5.  It is quite obvious that our attitudes about Sunday as a nation, city, and family have changed over the past 50-75 years.  How serious is this issue in our faith walk? Why? What action, if any, do you think we should take as committed Christians?

B6.  If we were Israel and considered "God's chosen people," violation of the Sabbath would be a serious violation of trust. But the USA is not a nation like Israel. We may have been founded on

Christian principles but we are a nation of diverse religions, not wholly a Christian nation founded by and dedicated to God or Christ in the same way or nature as Israel. Therefore, how do we approach questions like "keeping the Sabbath holy" in light of the diverse culture that exists today?

> Q. Do you think Sunday blue laws are appropriate? Why? Why not?

> Q. Do you think the US culture or society should be "inconvenienced" in any way by Christian practices?

> Q. What do you do if your employer requires you to work on Sunday?

B7. If you believe that the Sabbath rules apply to Sunday today, what would the following mean for you?
Isaiah 58:13-*14*      *"If you keep from desecrating the Sabbath, from doing whatever you want on My holy day; if you call the Sabbath a delight, and the holy day of the Lord honorable; if you honor it, not going your own ways, seeking your own pleasure, or talking too*

*much; 14 then you will delight yourself in the Lord, and I will make you ride over the heights of the land, and let you enjoy the heritage of your father Jacob." For the mouth of the Lord has spoken.*

## C. SABBATH RULES

A major temptation in our world today is to avoid obeying God's Word by compromising, through human reasoning, the requirements that apply to our lives. We may pay a high price with God, and experience spiritual disaster when we rewrite God's requirements out of our life. God may withdraw His presence, power and blessing, and may even bring discipline and judgment. The Sabbath is clearly important to God. The key question is, "*How important should it be to us*?" How much of it applies to the Christ-followers?

### *Are Christians to keep the Jewish Sabbath?*

In Colossians 2:16-17, the Apostle Paul declared, "Therefore do not let anyone judge you by what you eat or drink, or with regard to a religious festival, a New Moon celebration or a Sabbath day. These are a shadow of the things that were to come; the reality, however, is found in Christ."

Similarly, Romans 14:5 says, "One man considers one day more sacred than another; another man considers every day alike. Each one should be fully convinced in his own mind."

These Scriptures make it clear, for the Christian, Sabbath-keeping is a matter of spiritual freedom, not a command from God. Sabbath-keeping is an issue on which God's Word instructs us not to judge each other. Sabbath-keeping is a matter that each Christian needs to be fully convinced about in his or her own mind.

In the early chapters of the Book of Acts, the first Christians were predominantly Jews. When Gentiles began to receive the gift of salvation through Jesus Christ, the Jewish Christians had a dilemma. What aspects of the Mosaic Law and Jewish tradition should Gentile Christians be instructed to obey? The apostles met and discussed the issue in the Jerusalem council (Acts chapter 15). The decision was, "It is my judgment, therefore, that we should not make it difficult for the Gentiles who are turning to God. Instead we should write to them, telling them to abstain from food polluted by idols, from sexual immorality, from the meat of strangled animals and from blood" (Acts 15:19-20). Sabbath-keeping was not one of the commands that Jesus' apostles felt it was necessary to impose on Gentile believers. It is inconceivable that the apostles would neglect to include Sabbath-keeping if it was still God's command for Christians to observe the Sabbath day.

A common error in the Sabbath-keeping debate is the concept that the Sabbath was the day of worship. Groups such as the Seventh Day Adventists hold that God requires the church service to be held on Saturday, the Sabbath day. That is not what the Sabbath command was. The Sabbath command was to do no work on the Sabbath day (Exodus 20:8-11). Nowhere in Scripture is the Sabbath day commanded to be the day of worship. Yes, Jews in Old Testament, New Testament, and modern times use Saturday as the day of worship – but that is not the essence of the Sabbath command. In the Book of Acts, whenever a meeting is said to be on the Sabbath, it is a meeting of Jews, not Christians. When did the early Christians meet?

Acts 2:46-47 gives us the answer, "Every day they continued to meet together in the temple courts. They broke bread in their homes and ate together with glad and sincere hearts, praising God and enjoying the favor of all the people. And the Lord added to their number <u>daily</u> those who were being saved." If there was a day that Christians met regularly, it was the first day of the week, not the Sabbath day (Acts 20:7; 1 Corinthians 16:2). In honor of Christ's resurrection on Sunday, the early Christians observed Sunday, not as the "Christian Sabbath," but as a day to especially worship and glorify Jesus Christ.

Is there anything wrong with worshipping on Saturday, the Sabbath? Absolutely not! We should worship God every day, not just on Saturday or Sunday! Many churches today have both Saturday and Sunday services. There is freedom in Christ (Romans 8:21; 2 Corinthians 3:17; Galatians 5:1).

Should a Christian practice Sabbath-keeping, that is, not working on Saturdays? If a Christian feels led to do so, absolutely, yes (Romans 14:5). However, those who choose to practice Sabbath-keeping should not judge those who do not keep the Sabbath (Colossians 2:16). Further, those who do not keep the Sabbath should avoid being a stumbling block (1 Corinthians 8:9) to those who do keep the Sabbath. Galatians 5:13-15 sums up the whole issue, "You, my brothers, were called to be free. But do not use your freedom to indulge the sinful nature; rather, serve one another in love. The entire law is summed up in a single command: "Love your neighbor as yourself." If you keep on biting and devouring each other, watch out or you will be destroyed by each other."

Christians today have a degree of latitude in how they fulfill God's intentions for the Sabbath (Ro 14:5-13). But the spirit of "keeping the Sabbath holy" still means to honor God, to focus on the needs of others rather than ourselves, and to pursue fellowship, unity, and holiness. However, all days are to be dedicated to God through holy living.[1]

C1.  Do you agree with the above argument? Why? Why not?

C2.  If you agree with the above then how do you harmonize what Jesus says in Matthew 12:8, "*For the Son of Man is Lord of the Sabbath.*" What do you think this means for us today?

C3.  One thing is very clear, the Sabbath Day today is not part of the Law and it does not carry the necessity of absolute obedience in order to be "right with God." Therefore, we can agree that observing or not observing the Sabbath does not impact salvation. But keeping the Sabbath as a command of God to be "right with Him" is not the only reason or purpose of the "Sabbath." What are the other purposes of the Sabbath and what standing do they have today?

C4. Let's ignore all the obedience issues and special rules that tied Jewish believers to observing the Sabbath Law which produced a salvation situation for them – being right with God. What was the intent or spirit of what God wanted the Sabbath to do and be for His people and did that intent change with the advent of Jesus?

Intent: _____

Did it change: _____

## D.  APPLICATION

D1.  What impact could God have on your life if you truly made the Sabbath holy (totally dedicated to Him)?

D2.  Are you doing anything regularly or periodically on Sundays that dishonor or displease God?

D3.  Go back to question (A1) and review your answer. How would you change that answer now?

D4.  Is God pleased with how you observe Sunday? What do you do that would please God? What changes should you make?

## Personal Prayer:

*Lord,*

- Help me be true to Your plan for the Sabbath.
- Give me strength to honor You on Sunday.
- Allow me to keep Sunday holy and honor Your desires.
- Keep me from following the rules of men but rather follow Your rules.
- Assist me in being obedient to Your Word.
- I want to be holy as You are holy – help me, O Lord, to set Sunday aside for You.
- Lord, You know I have the habit of _____ on Sunday. Give me the ability to put that aside on Sunday and spend the day honoring You.
- I want to delight in You, Lord – help me to seek after You, focus on You, honor You . . .
- Give me the ability to celebrate You on Sunday, and make You my priority on Sunday.

AMEN

# *Shiphrah & Puah*
## midwives

---

**Occurrences of "Shiphrah and Puah" in the Bible:** 1
**Occurrences of "midwives:"** 6
(in relation to Shiphrah and Puah)

**Themes:** Obeying Man vs. Fearing God;
Life is Precious; Power Corrupts

---

## Scripture

Exodus 1:8-22

*Now there arose a new king over Egypt, who did not know Joseph.
9 And he said to his people, "Behold, the people of Israel are too
many and too mighty for us. 10 Come, let us deal shrewdly with
them, lest they multiply, and, if war breaks out, they join our
enemies and fight against us and escape from the land." 11
Therefore they set taskmasters over them to afflict them with
heavy burdens. They built for Pharaoh store cities, Pithom and
Raamses. 12 But the more they were oppressed, the more they
multiplied and the more they spread abroad. And the Egyptians
were in dread of the people of Israel. 13 So they ruthlessly made the
people of Israel work as slaves 14 and made their lives bitter with
hard service, in mortar and brick, and in all kinds of work in the
field. In all their work they ruthlessly made them work as slaves.*

*15 Then the king of Egypt said to the Hebrew midwives, one of whom was named Shiphrah and the other Puah, 16 "When you serve as midwife to the Hebrew women and see them on the birthstool, if it is a son, you shall kill him, but if it is a daughter, she shall live." 17 But the midwives feared God and did not do as the king of Egypt commanded them, but let the male children live. 18 So the king of Egypt called the midwives and said to them, "Why have you done this, and let the male children live?" 19 The midwives said to Pharaoh, "Because the Hebrew women are not like the Egyptian women, for they are vigorous and give birth before the midwife comes to them." 20 So God dealt well with the midwives. And the people multiplied and grew very strong. 21 And because the midwives feared God, he gave them families. 22 Then Pharaoh commanded all his people, "Every son that is born to the Hebrews you shall cast into the Nile, but you shall let every daughter live." ESV*

## The Context

The close of the Book of Genesis describes Joseph's life, his leadership in the nation of Egypt, and the reconciliation with his brothers. Joseph and his family stayed in Egypt after Jacob died and Joseph lived to see a third generation of his offspring. As Joseph was nearing death he told his brothers that God would rescue them and they would return to the Promised Land.

The Book of Exodus opens with a list of Jacob's sons and indicates that Joseph and all his brothers had died, but the original 70 descendants had multiplied greatly and become "exceedingly numerous." This became a great concern for the then current king in Egypt and he ordered the Hebrew people enslaved.

The story is leading toward the birth and rise of Moses as the Jewish leader who would lead his people out of Egypt. But first we learn that the king made an attempt to kill all new baby boys by enlisting the help of the midwives who assisted with the births of the Jewish women. Two of the midwives were Shiphrah and Puah. They may have been the leaders or managers over a number of other midwives.

Thus, we have the historical backdrop for Moses' rescue from the Nile by Pharaoh's daughter. Moses was born to a Jewish woman at this time and in a desperate attempt to save her son, put him in a sealed basket to float in the Nile. Moses was rescued from the Nile and became the adopted son of Pharaoh's daughter and ultimately led his people out of Egypt.

## Discussion Questions

A. GENERAL:

A1. Why do you think the new king "did not know about Joseph"? Do you think ignorance about history is a problem today?

A2. Why would the king think that the Jews would join the enemies of Egypt?

A3. Can you think of a similar occurrence in the history of the USA in the first half of the 20<sup>th</sup> century?

A4. What phrase is significant at the end of verse 1:10?

A5. Why do you think the king and other leaders thought oppression of this many people was a good idea? Why wouldn't love, patience, integration, openness, valuing, and rewarding etc. been a much better strategy?

A6. The names of Shiphrah and Puah are Semitic rather than Egyptian and 1:15 implies the midwives were Jewish. Why would the king think he could force these midwives to kill the babies of their own people?

A7.  What do you think was the king's ultimate goal? Did he want to eradicate the Jews?

A8.  The text only mentions two midwives. Do you think there were others?

A9.  Why would the king put the responsibility of his plan in the hands of the Jewish midwives rather than take some direct action himself?

A10.  Why did the midwives disobey the king?

A11.  Do you think the king really believed the midwives' lie? Why?

> Yes:

> No:

A12.  Why didn't the king try to determine the truth of the midwives claims? It would not have been that hard to determine if the story was true of false.

A13.  Why didn't the king immediately go about trying to kill baby boys in some other manner?

A14.  Do you think it would have been difficult to hide information about births from the Pharaoh?

A15.  What do you think were the Pharaoh's objectives?

A16.  What was different about the new order to throw the boy babies into the Nile?

A17.  Exodus 1:10 says the king wanted to deal shrewdly with the Israelites. What does *shrewdly* mean in this context?

A18.  Do you think the king acted shrewdly?




Q.  What would a shrewd king have done?




Q.  What are possible shrewd alternatives?




A19.  If the king wanted to control growth of the Israelite community and make them more subservient, was he successful?

## B. APPLICATION

B1. As a female mid-wife (or male doctor) what would have been your response to the king, if it had been you:

      a) today, and

      b) when you were age 20-25.


      Q.  Would you have lied to the king or been a "Daniel"?


B2. Have you ever secretly or shrewdly tried to avoid or reject God's laws? What happened? What did you learn?


B3. Other than "obeying God over man," what other life lessons do you see in this story?


B4. Have you ever worked for an employer who treated you ruthlessly or made your life bitter? What did you do about it? What should you have done about it? Why?

# *Lydia*
## dealer in purple cloth

---

**Occurrences of "Lydia" in the Bible:** 2

**Themes:** Spiritual Leadership; Listening; Revelation; Conversion and Baptism

---

## Scripture

Acts 16:11-15

*So, setting sail from Troas, we made a direct voyage to Samothrace, and the following day to Neapolis, 12 and from there to Philippi, which is a leading city of the district of Macedonia and a Roman colony. We remained in this city some days. 13 And on the Sabbath day we went outside the gate to the riverside, where we supposed there was a place of prayer, and we sat down and spoke to the women who had come together. 14 One who heard us was a woman named Lydia, from the city of Thyatira, a seller of purple goods, who was a worshiper of God. The Lord opened her heart to pay attention to what was said by Paul. 15 And after she was baptized, and her household as well, she urged us, saying, "If you have judged me to be faithful to the Lord, come to my house and stay." And she prevailed upon us.* ESV

## The Context

Prior to Paul's arrival in Philippi, Paul had been trying to travel to
Bithynia (16:7). But the text indicates that the Spirit of Jesus would
not allow Paul and his group to enter. We do not know the nature
of this warning or refusal by the Spirit, but Paul clearly felt, heard,
or saw the instruction not to proceed to Bithynia.

When the group reached Troas, Paul had a vision directing him to
Macedonia. Therefore they prepared at once to leave for
Macedonia. They boarded a ship and traveled to Philippi, a leading
city in one of Macedonia's four districts. Paul would establish
churches in Philippi, in the capital city of Thessalonica, and in
Thyatira, another nearby town which was Lydia's home.

## Background

Under the Jewish customs of that day a synagogue could be
formed only if there were 10 or more male heads of households.
When there were not enough male Jews to form a synagogue, it
was customary to gather at a "place of prayer" that was out in the
open air and near a river as an alternative. Since the Ganges River
was about 1.5 miles west of Philippi, that would be the first logical
place for Paul and Silas to look for the Jewish community given the
lack of a synagogue.[2]

Philippi, which today is located in northern Greece, was a key city
in the region. At that time Philippi was not open to unrecognized
religious gatherings in the city. Some commentaries and Bible study
notes suggest that there was a sign warning visitors that
unrecognized religious groups were not to meet in the city.[3]

The meeting outside of town ("place of prayer") was for Jews. Lydia
was a "worshipper of God" or a "God-fearer," meaning that she

was a Gentile follower of the Jewish faith, but not a full convert. The other women at the gathering were other Jews or "God-fearers" like Lydia. This gathering was taking place because of the absence of a synagogue.

## What Do We Know?

Paul was not traveling around the area and visiting friends, but rather was being led by the Spirit. And like other major characters of the Old Testament (Abraham for example), he and Silas immediately obeyed the Spirit, packed up their bags, and jumped on the first ship going toward Macedonia. The "No" he had been hearing that had been preventing him going to Bithynia had turned into a "Yes" for Macedonia.

The fact that Paul went looking for a "place of prayer" probably means that there were fewer than ten practicing Jewish families in Philippi. He met Lydia at this place of prayer. Later, Paul encountered a slave girl on his way to the same place. This encounter led to Paul and Silas' imprisonment. When they were released from prison, they went to Lydia's house where other believers were gathered. These believers may have included Lydia's household, visitors, and others traveling with Paul and Silas.

## Discussion Questions

### A. GENERAL

A1. Historically what was Paul's standard practice when he arrived at any new city?

A2.  Paul could have easily determined that there was no synagogue in the city. Why would he go outside the city gate looking for the local Jewish community?

A3.  Why would Paul wait until the Sabbath to go looking for the local Jewish community?

A4.  Who did Paul find at the place of prayer, and what is the significance?

A5.  Why do you suppose there were no men at the place of prayer?

A6.  How would you evaluate the spiritual condition of the small existing Jewish community in Philippi?

A7.  Why do you suppose the author indicates that Lydia is a dealer in purple cloth?

A8.  Acts 16:14 says that Lydia was a "worshipper of God." What does that mean or imply?

A9.  Acts 16:14 also says that the Lord "opened her heart." What does that mean?

A10.  Other than opening Lydia's heart to the Gospel, what else occurred because of what the Lord had done?

A11.  What is the evidence of Lydia's conversion?

A12.  Is there anything significant about the fact that the "household" was also baptized? What might this mean or imply?

A13.  Do you think the "household" really had saving faith?


A14.  What are the arguments for them having saving faith?


A15.  What role does baptism play in these events?


## ACTS 16:16-39


In Acts 16:16-39 the author reports the confrontation of the slave girl with a spirit who predicted the future which led to Paul and Silas' imprisonment. The last verse of chapter 16 says that Paul and Silas were released and went to Lydia's house:

Acts 16:38-40    *The police reported these words to the magistrates, and they were afraid when they heard that they were Roman citizens. 39 So they came and apologized to them. And they took them out and asked them to leave the city. 40 So they went out of the prison and visited Lydia. And when they had seen the brothers, they encouraged them and departed.* ESV

A16.  Why would Paul and Silas go to Lydia's house upon their release?

A17.  Who might have been the "brothers" at Lydia's house (16:40)?

A18.  One might suspect that after their release, Silas and Paul would want to relax and recover. But what happened?

## B. APPLICATION

B1.  SPIRITUAL RESPONSIBILITY: In Western society men have often abdicated their responsibility as the spiritual heads of their families:

> B1a.  Men: Have you neglected, in any way, your responsibility as the spiritual head of your family?

> B1b.  Women: Have you allowed the spiritual failure of a husband or father to impact your spiritual life?

B2.  Do you know anyone who has been baptized but shows no sign of having saving faith?

B3.  Do you know anyone who should participate in believer's baptism? What could you do to help?

B4.  Lydia was listening and paying attention. How about you? Is the Lord speaking to you? How do you know? Are you listening? Are you paying attention?

B5.  Do you know anyone as dedicated to their Christian mission as Paul and Silas were?

      a.  What drives or motivates them?

      b.  Is their dedication contagious?

# Now What?

### *Get Wisdom – General Information:*

**www.getwisdompublishing.com**

### *Get Wisdom – Resources:*
You can access free resources from Get Wisdom by going to:

**www.getwisdom.link/resources**

### *Grace and the Gravel Road:*
Grace & the Gravel Road teaches both the Truth+Tools that Christ-followers need to fully live the life God has for them.

**www.graceandthegravelroad.com**

### *You Can Help:*
Mention The *OBSCURE* Bible Study Series on your social platforms. Include the hashtag #obscureBiblestudy so we are aware of your post.

Recommend *OBSCURE* to your family, friends, small group, Sunday School class leaders, or your church.

*Thanks so much!*

# The *OBSCURE* Bible Study Series

### Meet Shamgar, Jethro, Manoah & Hathach
**An introduction to the OBSCURE Bible Study Series.**

This book of four lessons is provided at a reduced cost so that students and leaders can get a first-hand experience and introduction to The *OBSCURE* Bible Study Series.

### Blasphemy, Grace, Quarrels & Reconciliation
**The intriguing lives of first-century disciples.**

This book presents Joseph of Arimathea, Joanna, Ananias, Hymenaeus, and Cornelius (a centurion). It illustrates the nature and challenges of life as a first-century disciple. Life has real challenges, but they can be overcome.

### The Beginning and the End
**From creation to eternity.**

This book has four lessons from Genesis and four from the book of Revelation. It covers such topics as creation, rebellion, grace, worship, and eternity. It illustrates how God is leading us to worship in the Throne Room.

### God at the Center
**He is sovereign and I am not.**

This book examines the virgin birth, worship, prayer, the sovereignty of God, compromise, and trust. God is at the center of all these stories. He is there in the shadows or openly orchestrating our lives. Regardless of the situation He is at the center of our lives – a sovereign almighty God.

### Women of Courage
**God did some serious business with these women.**

This book examines the lives of Jael, Rizpah, the woman of Tekoa, Tabitha, Shiphrah, and Lydia. We see these women exhibiting great courage and faithfulness. God used them in amazing ways and we can use their example for encouragement and spiritual leadership.

### The Beginning of Wisdom
**Your personal character counts.**

In this book we find courage, loyalty, thankfulness, love, forgiveness, and humility. Personal character counts. It is critical to make good decisions because they have consequences. Building our lives on wisdom will help us stand firm in our faith. We should reject the example of Demas who deserted Paul for the values of the world.

### Miracles & Rebellion
**The good, the bad, and the indifferent.**

This book contrasts characters who rebelled against God with those who trusted in Him. God hates sin and loves to heal the faithful. The rebellion of Korah, Haman, and Alexander are included to compare with the healing stories of Aeneas, a slave girl, and the crippled man at Lystra.

### The Chosen People
**There is a remnant.**

This book concentrates mostly on Israel in the Old Testament, but also covers some interesting subjects as Lucifer, Michael the archangel, and Job's wife.

### The Chosen Person
**Keep your eyes on Jesus.**

The focus of this book is on Jesus and the superiority of Christ. We investigate Melchizedek, the disciples on the road to Emmaus, Nicodemus, the criminal on the cross who asks to be remembered by Jesus, and others.

# Acknowledgments

### *Arlene*
Arlene has served as wife, editor, and proof-reader for all of my writing – thank you for your patience, help, and love.

### *Michelle*
Michelle, our older daughter, has been an invaluable resource. She has graciously produced the website at www.getwisdompublishing.com. She was the first author in the family: graceandthegravelroad.com.

### *Stephanie*
Our middle daughter designed all the covers for the *OBSCURE* Bible Study Series, as well as the marks and logos for Get Wisdom Publishing. We are grateful for her talent!

### *KOINONIA Small Group*
These dear friends have hung in there with me as I taught many of the lessons to them first. Their input, answers, and suggestions have been invaluable.

### *God, Jesus, and Holy Spirit*
Thank you, Lord, for Your guidance and direction.

# Notes

1    Bible Questions Answered: www.GotQuestions.org; *Got Questions*, Answers to the Questions People are Really Asking: Are Christians to keep the Jewish Sabbath? S. Michael Houdmann, General Editor. ISBN 978-1-4908-3273-9, page 202.

2    Zondervan NIV Bible Commentary, Volume 2: New Testament, page 470-471.

3    Tyndale's Life Application Study Bible (NLT) study notes for Acts 16:11-20, page 1860-1867.

# About the Author

Steve attended church as a child and accepted Christ when he was 10 years old. But his walk with Jesus left a lot to be desired for the next 44 years. In 1994 he "wrestled" with God for some period of months and in September of that year totally surrendered his life to Jesus.

In 1996 he was so driven to study God's Word that he attended the Indianapolis campus of Trinity Evangelical Divinity School (Chicago) to earn a Certificate of Biblical Studies. His hunger for God's Word led him to lead and write all his own Bible studies for his small group. He has been an entrepreneur and Bible study leader for the past 25 years.

In 2019 he was one of four members who founded The Acanthus Group (www.theacanthusgroup.org). He is a member of The Church at Station Hill in Spring Hill, TN, a regional campus of Brentwood Baptist (Brentwood TN).

**www.getwisdompublishing.com**

# *Key Points To Remember*

*Record ideas, thoughts, and concepts you want to remember.*

_____

_____

_____

_____

_____

_____

_____

_____

_____

_____

_____

_____

_____

_____

_____

Made in the USA
Middletown, DE
07 July 2021

43774216R00076